THUNDER ENTERED HER

Thunder entered her –
And made no sound;
There entered the Shepherd of all,
And in her He became
The Lamb, bleating as he comes forth.

Nativity Hymn No. 11
by St Ephrem the Syrian

Ἀμην.   Ameen.   *Amen.*

Refrain:
Величаемъ Тя.   Velichayem Iya.   *We magnify you.*

Nativity Hymn No. 11 by St Ephrem the Syrian

*Translation is here set to music and reproduced by kind permission of
Dr Sebastian Brock and the fellowship of St Alban and St Sergius*

CONTEMPORARY CHURCH MUSIC SERIES

JOHN TAVENER

THUNDER ENTERED HER

FOR SATB CHORUS, TB SEMICHORUS, HANDBELL AND ORGAN

CHESTER MUSIC

This work was commissioned by the St Albans Chamber Choir with financial support from Eastern Arts Association. It was first performed on 15th June 1991 at St Albans Abbey, by the St Albans Chamber Choir conducted by Richard Stangroom.

Duration: c. 20 minutes

Score available on sale: Order No. CH59584

SCORING

SATB chorus

Separate, small group of male voices and handbell , which should be placed as far as possible from the main choir

Organ

COMPOSER'S NOTE

Thunder Entered Her is a divine allegory which ponders on the mystery of the Incarnation as described by St Ephrem the Syrian, the greatest poet of the patristic age, and perhaps the only theologian poet to rank beside Dante. So rich is the symbolism of St Ephrem's poetry that he said, slightly ironically, "Jesus, you have so many symbols, I am drowning in a sea of them". He died in 373 in Edessa (Urfa, east of the Euphrates in modern south-east Turkey), a town which was for a long time the spiritual home of Syriac-speaking Christianity.

The salvation effected by Christ's residing in Mary's womb, in the 'womb' of Jordan, and in the 'womb' of the grave, is seen as being already fully accomplished in the temporal event of the feast. In liturgical time, past, present and future are all conjoined in an eternal 'now'.

J.T.

for Charlotte

THUNDER ENTERED HER

John Tavener (1990)

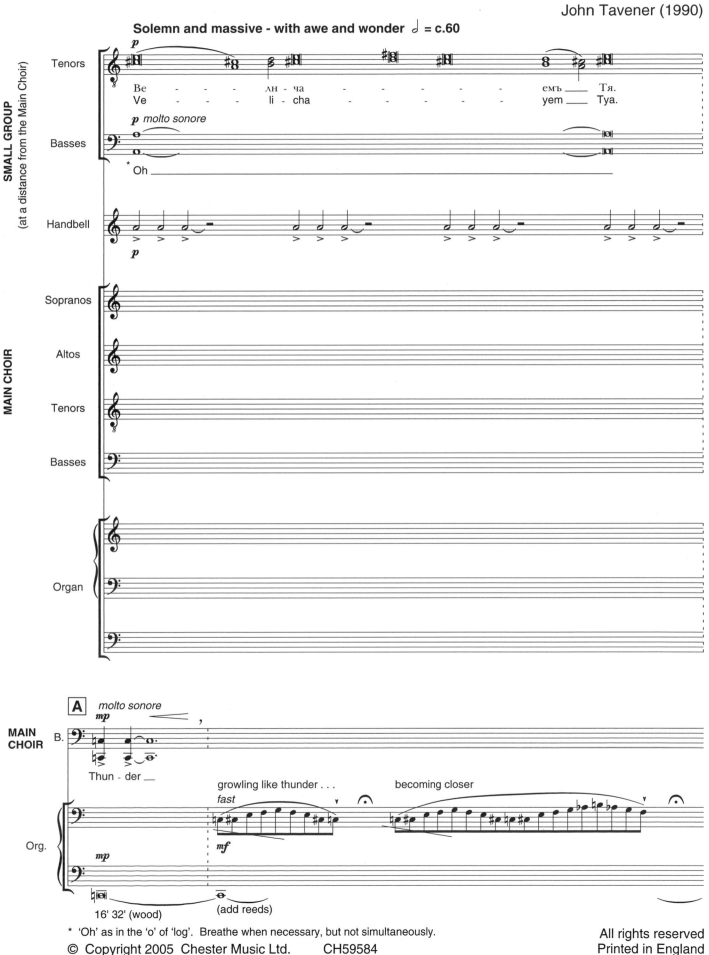

Solemn and massive - with awe and wonder ♩ = c.60

* 'Oh' as in the 'o' of 'log'. Breathe when necessary, but not simultaneously.

2

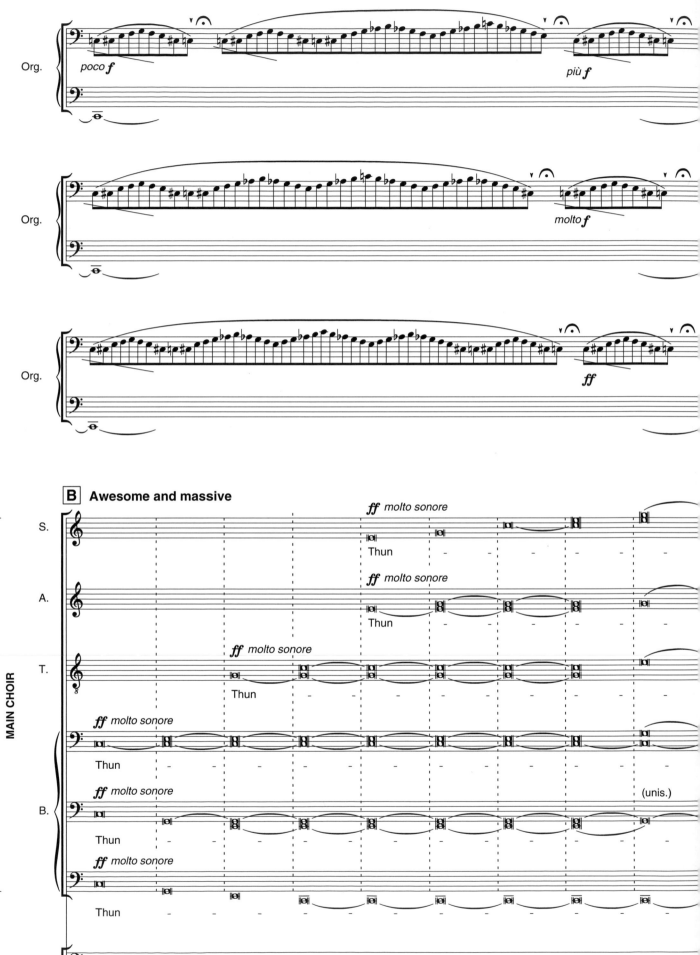

4

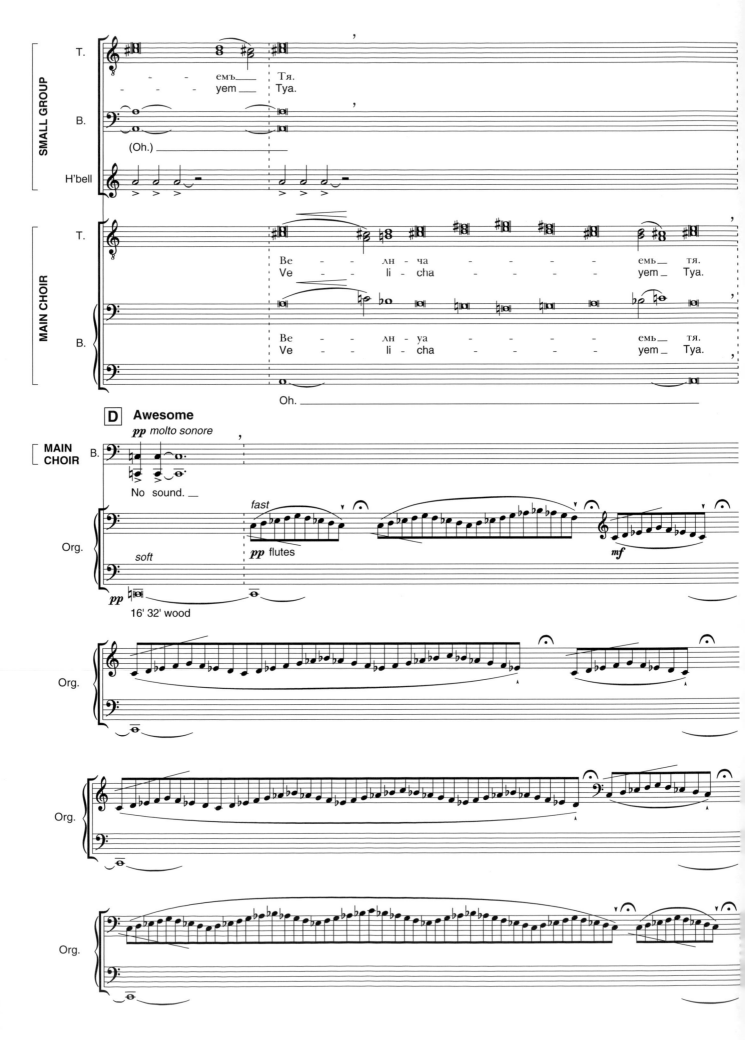

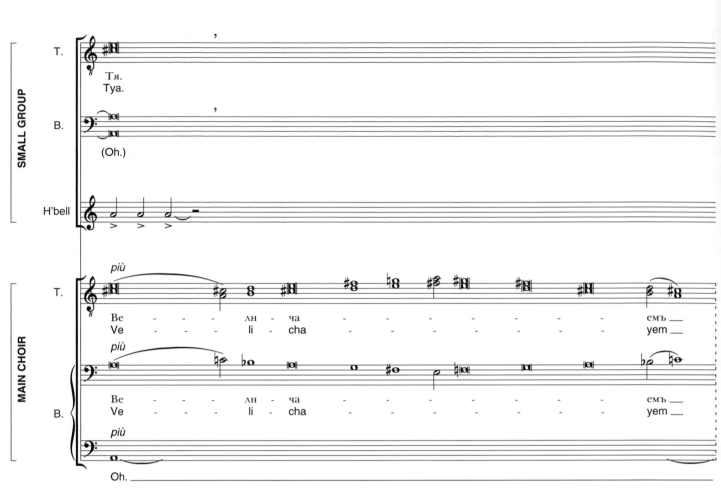

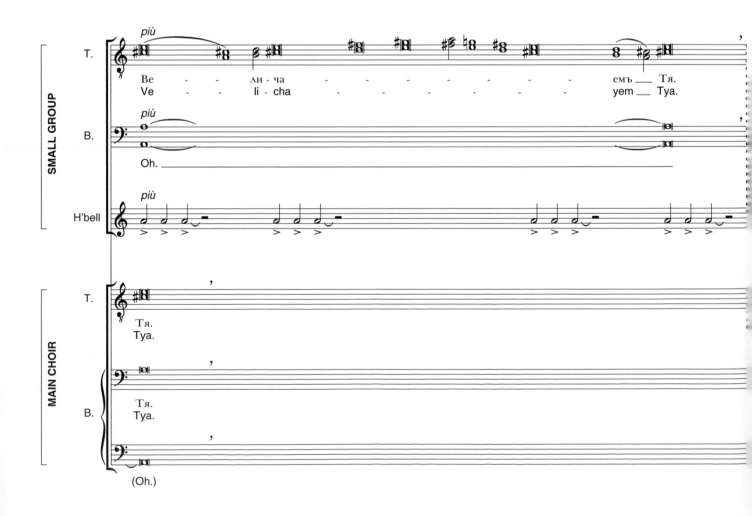

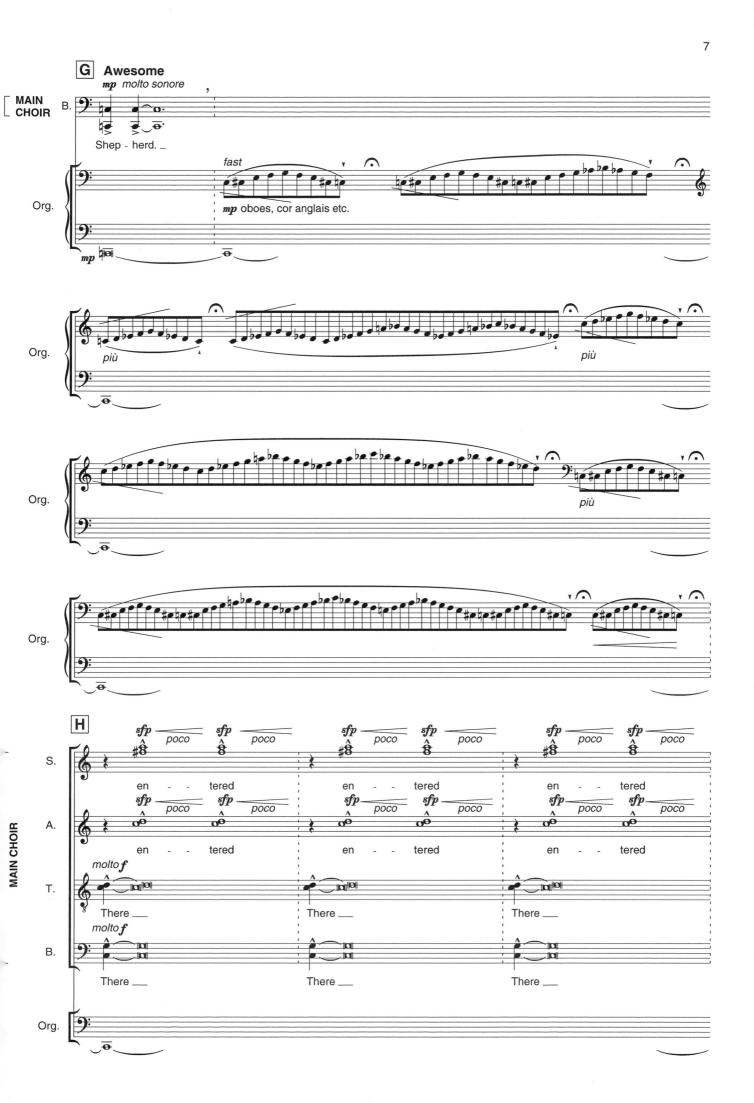

8

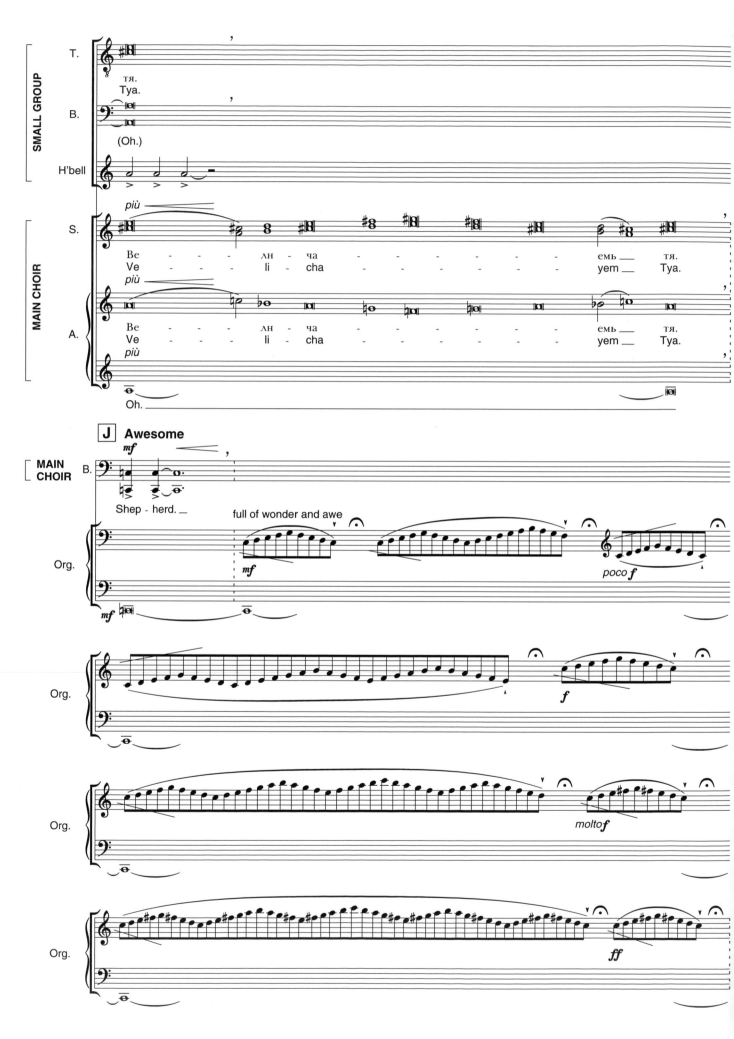

mp tierce fifteenth 8' 2'

Org.

K Legato

MAIN CHOIR

S.

And   in

A - - μην. A - - μην. A - - μην. A - - μην.
A - - meen. A - - meen. A - - meen. A - - meen.

A.

And   in

A - - μην. A - - μην. A - - μην. A - - μην.
A - - meen. A - - meen. A - - meen. A - - meen.

T.

Oh.

B.

Oh.

Org.

12

coming into sharp focus

MAIN CHOIR

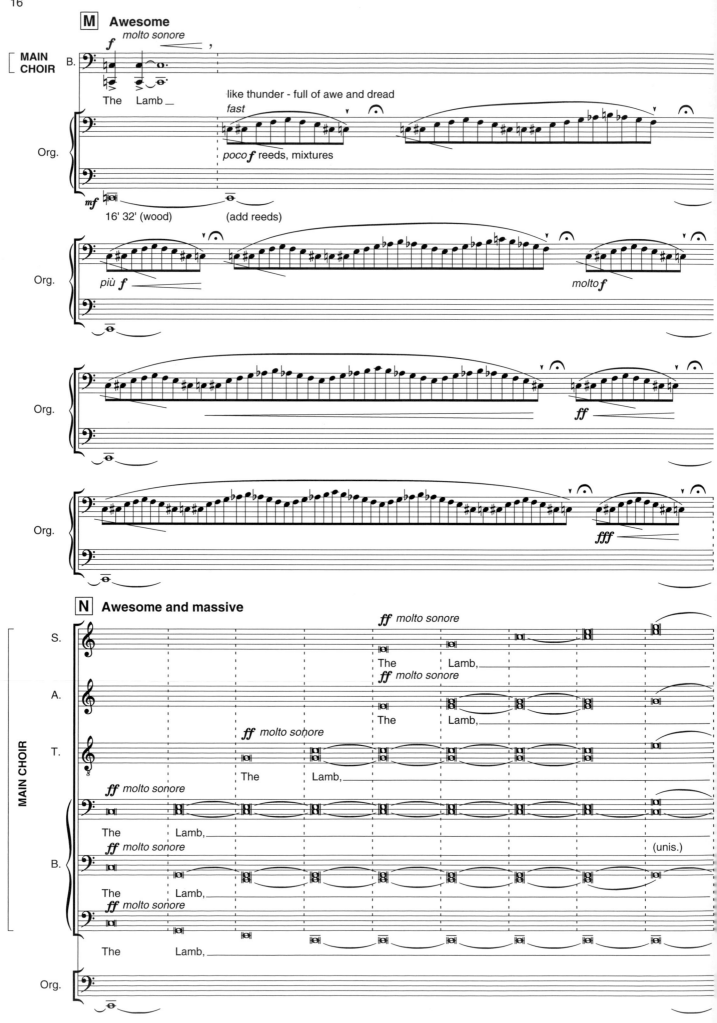

18

O The Sacrificial Lamb

* ⅓ denotes a microtone, a characteristic 'break in the voice' of Byzantine chant.
† If a tenor soloist is not available, this part may be sung an octave higher by a soprano.

Nafsika
Aegina, Greece
28th June 199

2 3 4 5 6 7 8 9

Selected choral works by
JOHN TAVENER

Unaccompanied choir, and choir with organ

The Lamb (1982)

Two Hymns to the Mother of God (1985)

Magnificat and Nunc Dimittis (1986)

Song for Athene (1993)

As one who has slept (1996)

Funeral Canticle (1996)

Birthday Sleep (1999)

Butterfly Dreams (2002)

Exhortation and Kohima (2003)

Missa Brevis (2005)
for treble voices (or SATB chorus) and organ

Choral works with orchestra/ensemble

Ultimos Ritos (1972)
for soloists, children's chorus, SATB chorus and orchestra

Resurrection (1989)
for soloists, chorus and orchestra

Fall and Resurrection (1997)
for soloists, chorus and orchestra

Lamentations and Praises (2000)
for twelve solo voices (or chorus) and instrumental ensemble

Ikon of Eros (2000)
for violin, soprano and baritone soloists, chorus and orchestra

The Veil of the Temple (2002)
all-night vigil for soloists, chorus and instrumental ensemble

CHESTER MUSIC

part of The Music Sales Group
14–15 Berners Street,
London W1T 3LJ, UK.

EXCLUSIVELY
DISTRIBUTED BY
HAL LEONARD
CORPORATION
14032894
U.S. $9.95

8 84088 42512 8

Order No. CH59584
ISBN 978-1-84609-398-2

9 781846 093982